LIFE CYCLE OF A
JELLYFISH

By Kirsty Holmes

KidHaven
PUBLISHING

LIFE CYCLES

Published in 2022 by
KidHaven Publishing, an Imprint of Greenhaven Publishing, LLC
353 3rd Avenue
Suite 255
New York, NY 10010

Edited by: Robin Twiddy
Designed by: Brandon Mattless

Find us on

Cataloging-in-Publication Data

Names: Holmes, Kirsty.
Title: Life cycle of a jellyfish / Kirsty Holmes.
Description: New York : KidHaven Publishing, 2022. | Series: Life cycles | Includes glossary and index.
Identifiers: ISBN 9781534537866 (pbk.) | ISBN 9781534537880 (library bound) | ISBN 9781534537873 (6 pack) | ISBN 9781534537897 (ebook)
Subjects: LCSH: Jellyfishes--Juvenile literature. | Jellyfishes--Life cycles--Juvenile literature.
Classification: LCC QL375.6 H68 2022 | DDC 593.5'3156--dc23

Printed in the United States of America

CPSIA compliance information: Batch #CSKH22: For further information contact Greenhaven Publishing LLC, New York, New York at 1-844-317-7404.

Please visit our website, www.greenhavenpublishing.com. For a free color catalog of all our high-quality books, call toll free 1-844-317-7404 or fax 1-844-317-7405.

Words that look like **this** can be found in the glossary on page 24.

PHOTO CREDITS

All images are courtesy of shutterstock.com, unless otherwise specified.
With thanks to Getty Images, Thinkstock Photo and iStockphoto. Front cover & 1 – Eric Isselee, Andrey_Kuzmin. 2 – Luis Miguel Casado. 3 – Andrey_Kuzmin. 4 – sirtravelalot, Gelpi, 2xSamara.com. 5 – Darrin Henry, mimagephotography, Hogan Imaging. 6 – Eric Isselee. 7 – Maxfield Weakley. 8 – aaltair. 9 – fboudrias. 10 – SrjT. 11 – Damsea. 12 – stephan kerkhofs. 13 – Dogora Sun. 14 – Ethan Daniels. 15 – HunterKitty. 16 – bierchen. 17 – Janos Rautonen. 18 – RaDoll, Ethan Daniels, Jiri Vaclavek, Love the wind. 19 – Dewald Kirsten, Doug McLean. 20 – Richard Whitcombe. 21 – scubadesign. 22 – fboudrias, SrjT, stephan kerkhofs. 23 – Dogora

CONTENTS

Baby

Toddler

Child

All living things have a life cycle. They are born, they all grow bigger, and their bodies change.

Adult

When they are fully grown, they have **offspring** of their own. In the end, all living things die. This is the life cycle.

Elderly Person

JOYFUL JELLYFISH

A jellyfish is an **invertebrate**. Jellyfish have no brain, bones, or heart. They are made up of a smooth body, which looks like a bag, and most have long tentacles.

Jellyfish use their **oral** tentacles to feed.

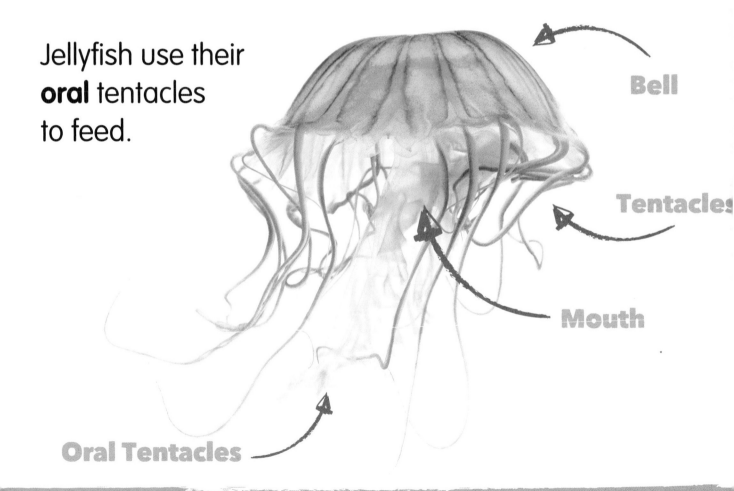

Bell

Tentacles

Mouth

Oral Tentacles

Look closely. Can you see the stinger **cells** on this tentacle?

Jellyfish tentacles are covered in small stinger cells. These cells have **venom** in them and they can sting or even kill other animals. Jellyfish can shoot water from their mouths to push them forward.

EXCITING EGGS

The moon jellyfish **fertilizes** its eggs on its arms.

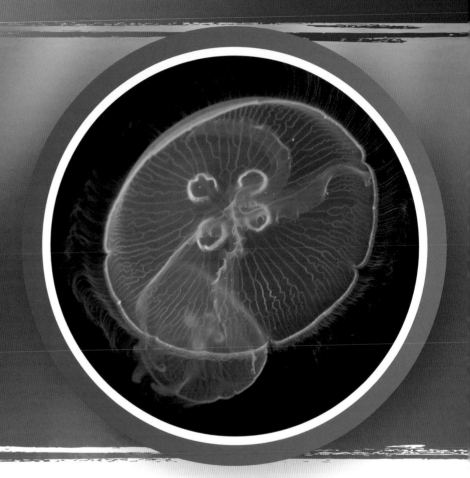

The male and female jellyfish mix their **sperm** and eggs together so that they become fertilized. Different species of jellyfish have different ways to do this. Some release them into the water to mix them.

Some jellyfish fertilize the eggs in the mother's mouth or a special pouch called a brood pouch. Other jellyfish fertilize their eggs in the water and let them float away.

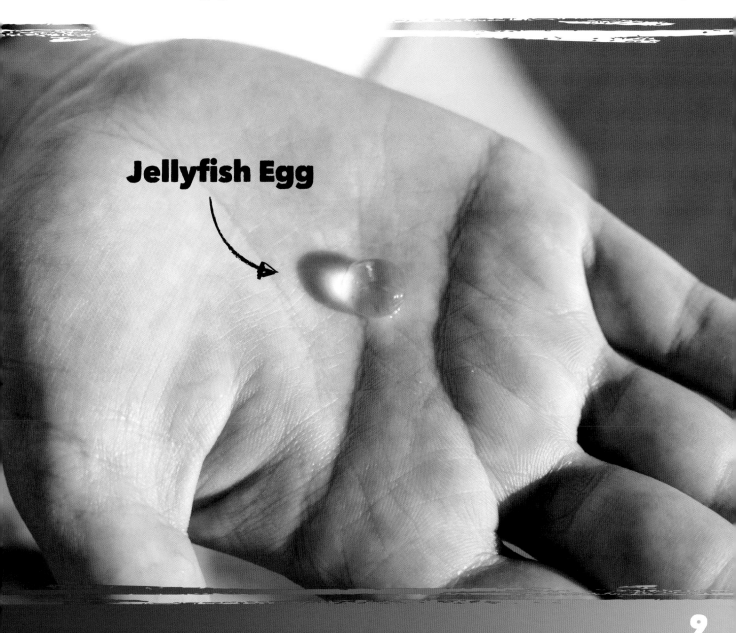

Jellyfish Egg

LIVELY LARVAE

The eggs then develop into **larvae**, called planulae, which can swim. They are shaped a little like a flat pear.

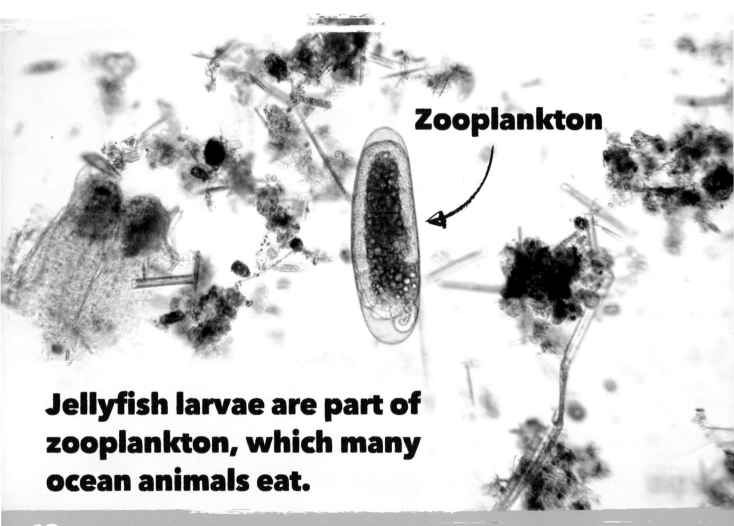

Zooplankton

Jellyfish larvae are part of zooplankton, which many ocean animals eat.

The planula slowly drops toward the bottom of the sea. It will eventually attach itself to a rock or another solid surface before becoming a polyp.

PERFECT POLYPS

The polyps may multiply so there are lots of them. This is called a colony. The polyps then become **dormant** while they wait for everything around them to be just right.

Polyp Colony

When they are ready, the polyps bud. This means that they release tiny baby jellyfish. These baby jellyfish are called ephyrae. They take a few weeks to become full-grown jellyfish.

JIGGLING JELLYFISH!

Adult jellyfish have fully developed bodies. Their tentacles grow, and so does the main part of their body, the bell. The jellyfish get bigger.

The bell of the lion's mane jellyfish can grow to almost 6 feet (2 m) across.

Adult jellyfish can have offspring of their own. All jellyfish look different. Some have really long tentacles, and some have really short ones. Some jellyfish can even glow!

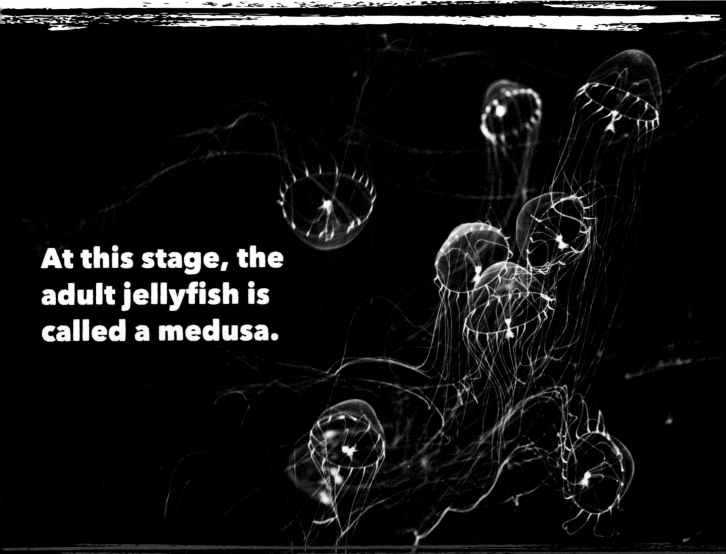

At this stage, the adult jellyfish is called a medusa.

LIFE AS A JELLYFISH

Jellyfish are **carnivores**. They use their stinging tentacles to sting and catch their **prey**. Jellyfish float around in the sea, and some use their mouth and bell to move around.

There are over 2,000 types of jellyfish and they can be found all over the world. They all look different and can come in a lot of different colors too.

FUN FACTS ABOUT JELLYFISH

• The Mediterranean jellyfish looks like a fried egg.

• Sometimes there can be a LOT of jellyfish at once in a small area. When this happens, it is called a jellyfish bloom. Blooms can even break boats!

• Jellyfish are about nine-tenths water.

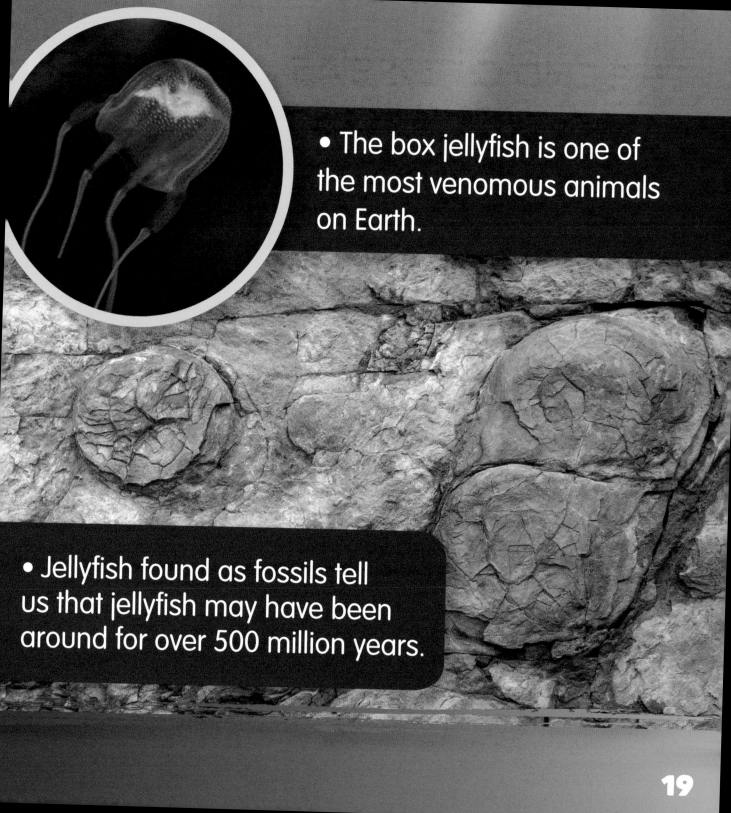

- The box jellyfish is one of the most venomous animals on Earth.

- Jellyfish found as fossils tell us that jellyfish may have been around for over 500 million years.

THE END OF LIFE AS A JELLYFISH

This species doesn't have tentacles.

Surprisingly, despite the stinging tentacles, lots of creatures think a jellyfish is a tasty treat. Sea turtles, sunfish, other jellyfish, and even people catch and eat jellyfish if they can.

One species of jellyfish might be able to live forever. The immortal jellyfish can go back to the polyp stage and start its adult life again.

The immortal jellyfish can still die if eaten.

THE LIFE CYCLE

Egg

Polyp

Planula

The life cycle of a jellyfish has different stages.
Each stage looks very different from the last.

Ephyra

In the end, the jellyfish dies and the life cycle is complete.

Adult

The male fertilizes the female's eggs. When the planulae hatch, they find a safe spot to attach themselves to and become polyps. Polyps release tiny jellyfish, called ephyrae, which grow into adults.

GLOSSARY

carnivore — an animal that eats other animals rather than plants

cell — the basic building block that makes up all living things

dormant — not active

fertilize — to join sperm with an egg

invertebrate — an animal without a backbone

larvae — young animals that must grow and change form before they become adults

offspring — the young of an animal or plant

oral — having to do with the mouth

prey — animals that are hunted by other animals for food

sperm — the cell made by the male of a species that fertilizes a female egg

venom — a harmful substance that is injected through a sting

INDEX